"This is a must read for anyone wanting to learn more about the copyright process."

Anthony Hester, Owner
Award Winning BBQ TEAM
www.cookingwithuncletony.com

The One Hour Copyright ©

by Anthony D. Hester

The One Hour Copyright ©

Copyright © 2012

Acknowledgments

Special thanks to my family and friends.

Most people have good intentions when buying a (200 pages) thick book thinking that they have everything that they need to accomplish their goals. However, they realize ten years later that the book has an inch of dust on it and their intellectual idea is still just a ten-year-old idea.

This book is titled, "The One Hour Copyright." Time results will vary based on the end users computer knowledge. Make sure you have all of the necessary documents (paper/electronic/Visa or Check) available to complete the copyright process in a short period of time.

Note: The One Hour Copyright is just a tool used to accomplish the end goal of a Copyright. This book is not designed to be the official source for a Copyright. This book was not designed to be the official source for legal advice or to replace the knowledge of a licensed Attorney in your state.

How long does a copyright last? The term of copyright for a particular work depends on several factors, including whether it has been published, and, if so, the date of first publication. As a general rule, for works created after January 1, 1978, copyright protection lasts for the life of the author plus an additional 70 years.

Please visit the Copyright Office official website for more instructions and guidance.

www.copyright.gov

Phone: 1-877-476-0778 (toll free)

Office hours 8:30 a.m. to 5:00 p.m. Eastern Time, Monday – Friday

1) Go to http://www.copyright.gov

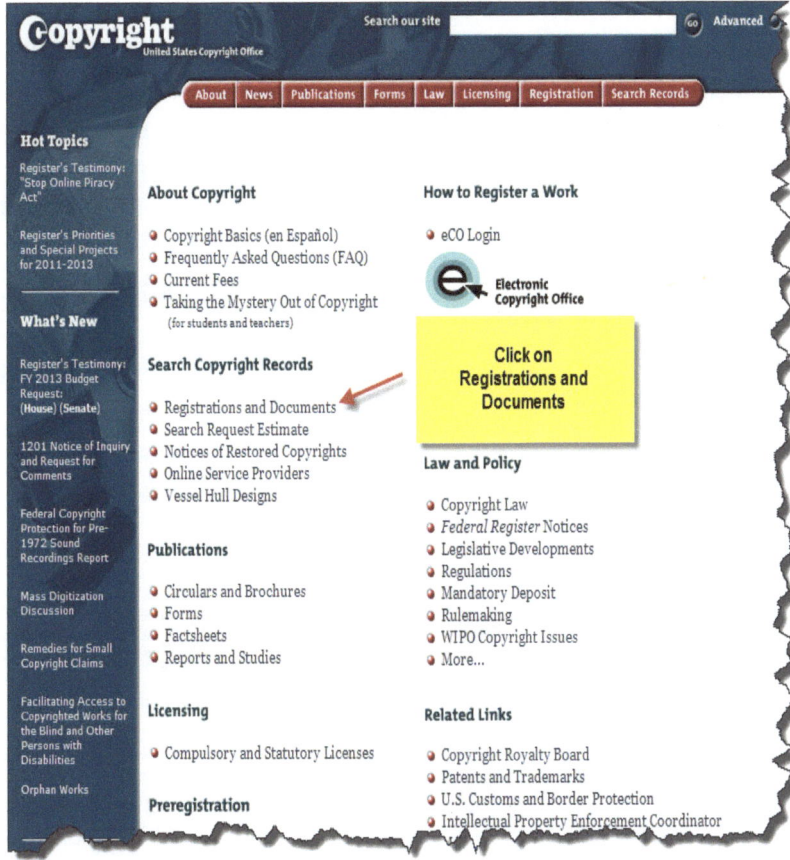

2) Go to the section that says search copyright records.

*Note: anything with a red asterisk must be filled in.

3) Click on Registration and Documents

4) Click on the Search and Catalog link

5) After typing your title in the search box make sure it's spelled right. The search is only as good as the information that you tell the computer to search.

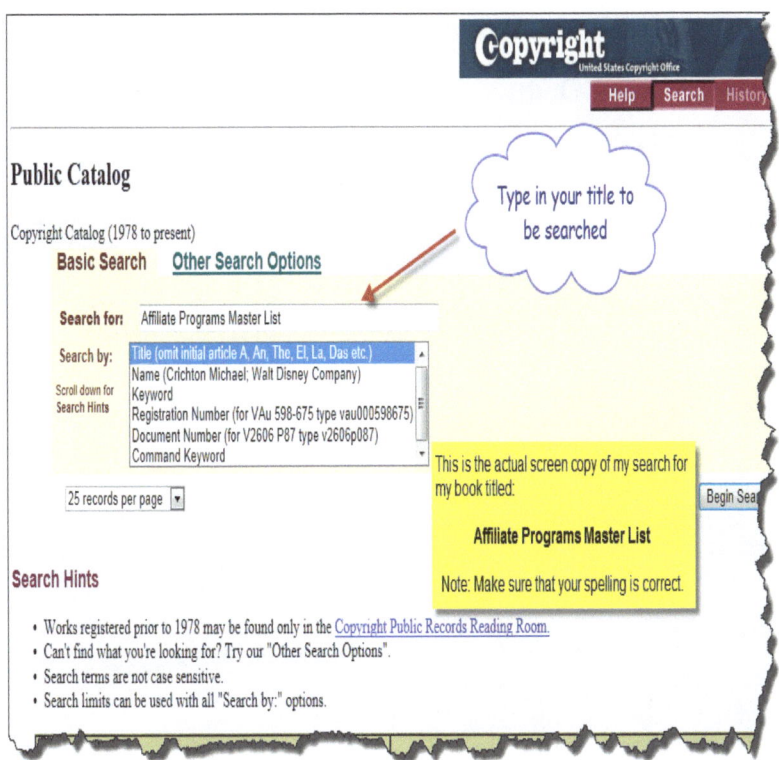

*Note:

When you see the words that say, that your search found no results you know it's time to copyright your product name/title. The book that I wrote titled, The Affiliate Programs Master List Volume One made from the screen shots in this book has been approved. Please visit Amazon.com and buy your copy today!

Book Link: http://tinyurl.com/d48enfp

Now back to the important stuff, let's finish this copyright.

File for a new project title.

6) Go back to the homepage.

7) Click on eCO login

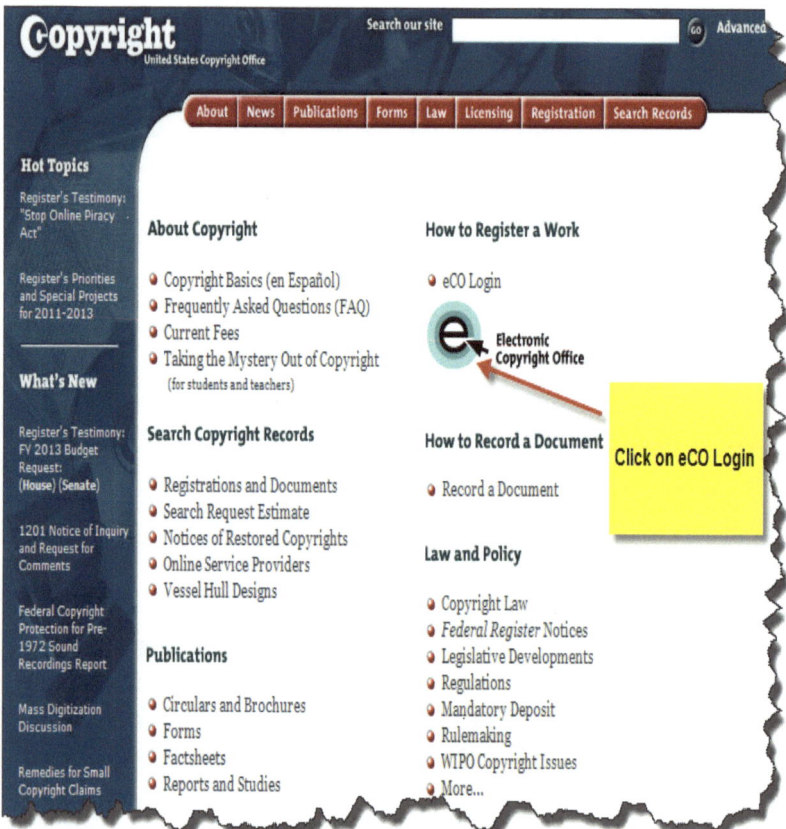

8) Click on the words, Electronic Copyright Office.

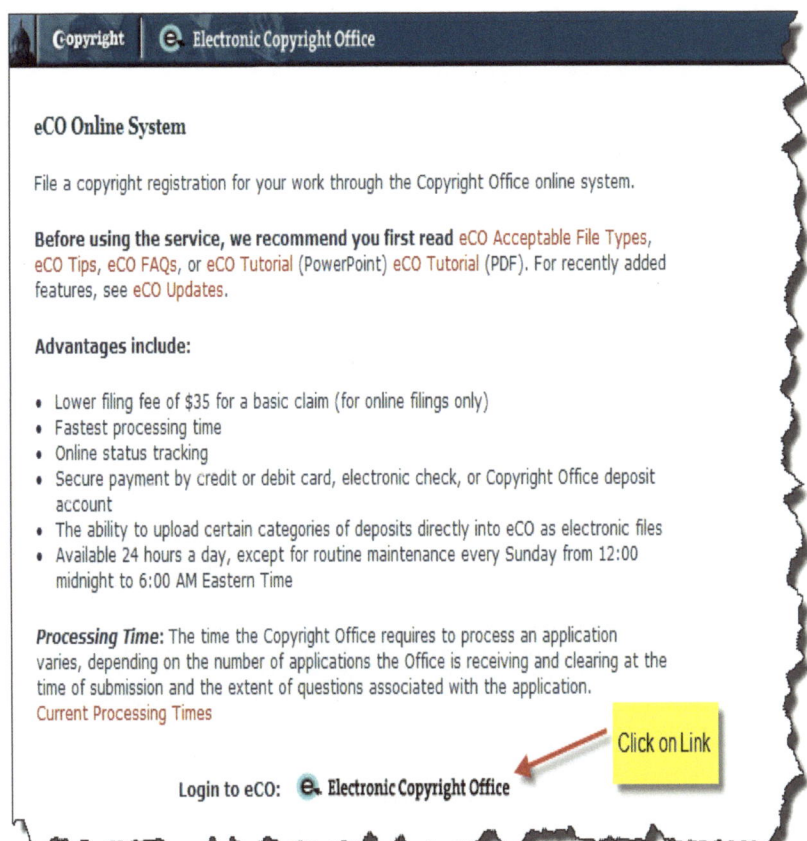

9) After reading the statement on the next page click on the, Continue to eCO button.

10) Next click on the new users section.

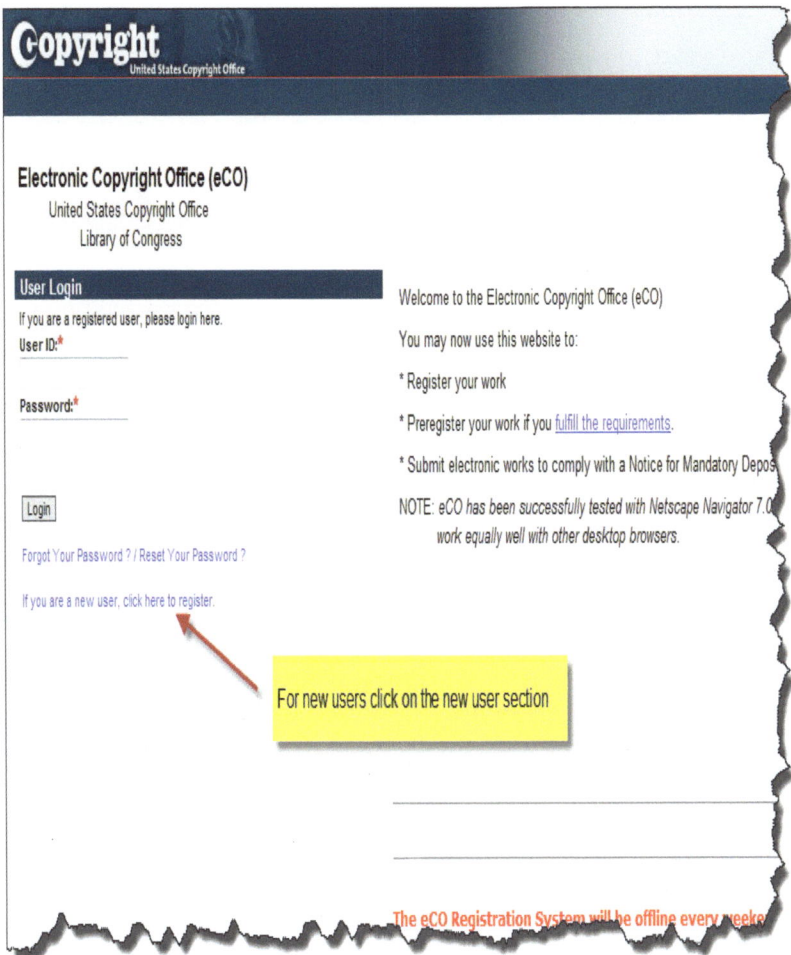

11) After clicking on the new users account register your information.

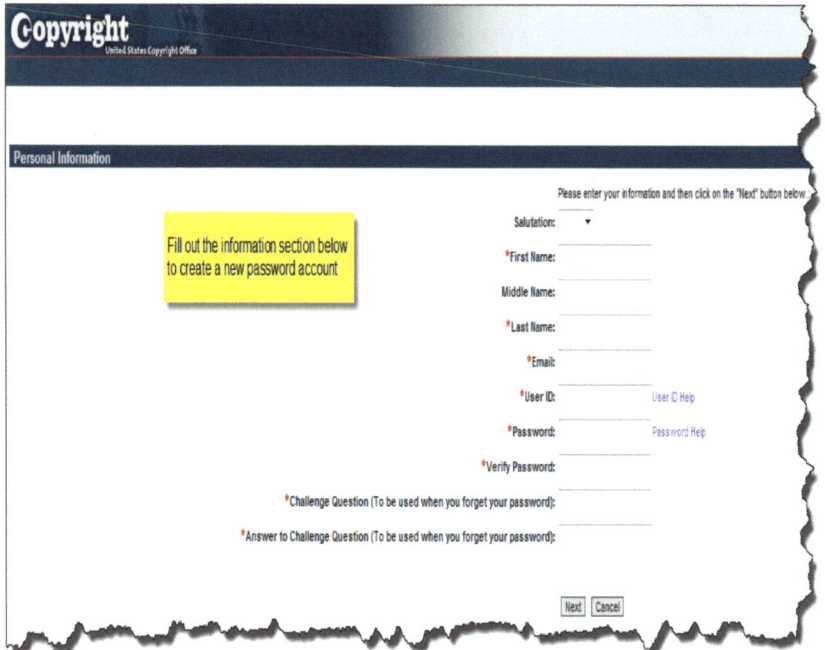

12) After you set up your password you will login on the below screen anytime to edit your work.

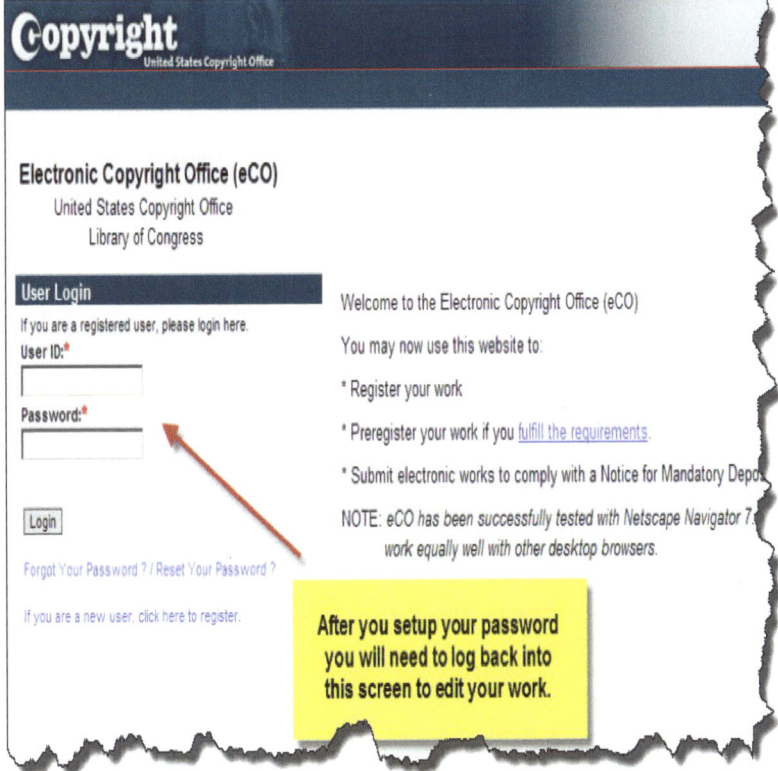

13) It's time to start a new copyright. Click on the Start Registration button.

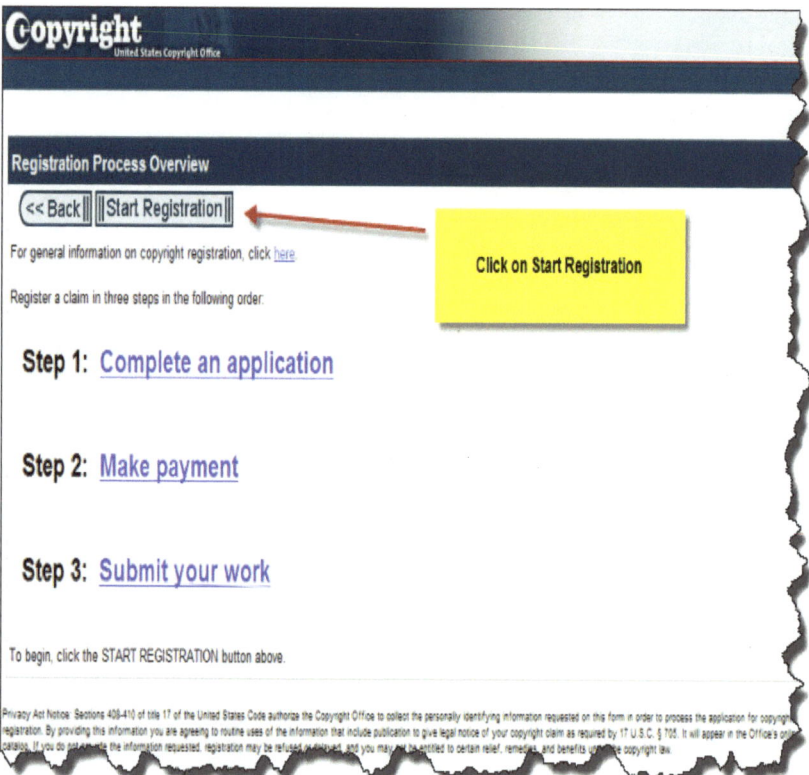

14) On this screen you must choose the type of work that you need to register. If you have any question click on the information listed below for definitions.

Once your ready click on the, Type of work drop down arrow.

Note: Information cannot be changed after making your selection.

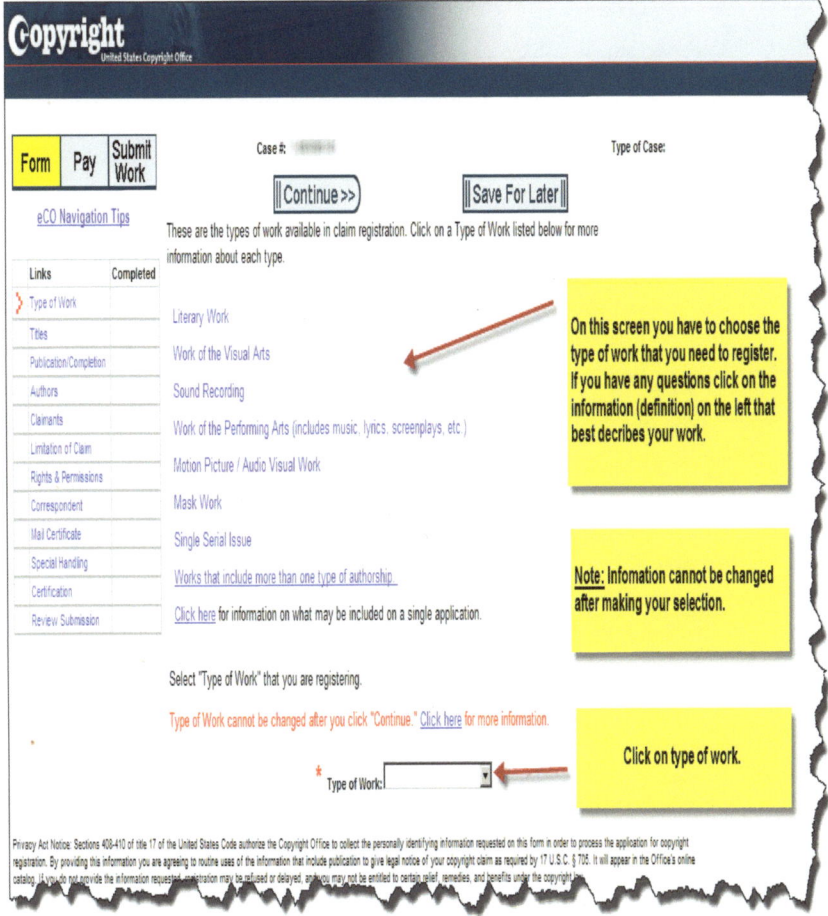

Notes:
- Your case number is located at the top of the screen.
- You can click on the save button to continue your work at a later time.
- Always stay in the habit of hitting the save button while working on the copyright.

15) Click on the continue button and the Titles screen will be next task. Click on the New button to create a new title.

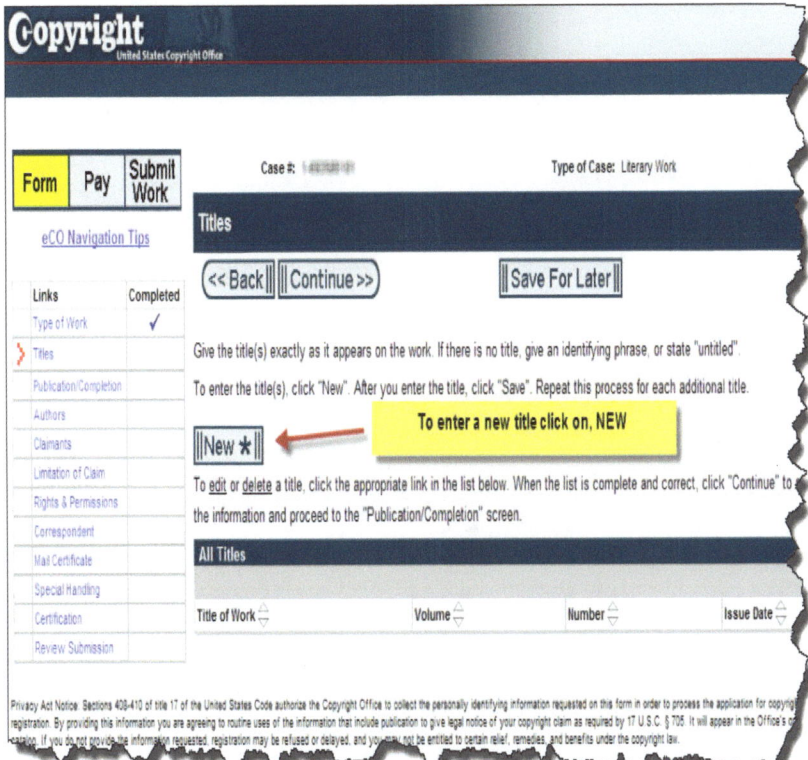

Copyright © 2012, Anthony D. Hester

16) During this section select a Title for your project and click save.

Note: If your books are going to be part of a Series please select the, Series Title option.

17) After you insert your title check over your work then click, Continue.

Note: If you have any changes click on the pencil to edit the Title.

18) Click Save.

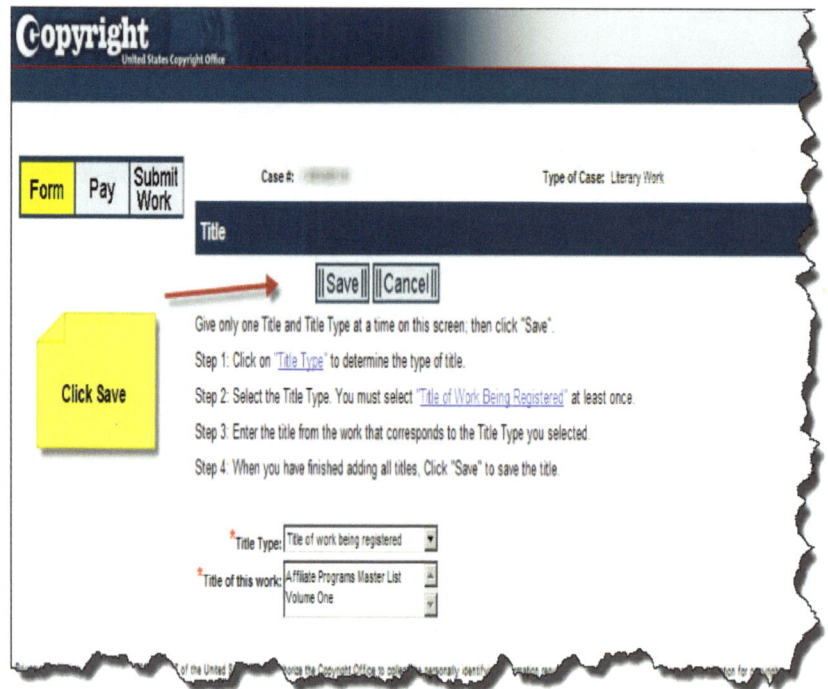

19) If your work has been published check Yes or No. Enter the Year of completion and click, Continue.

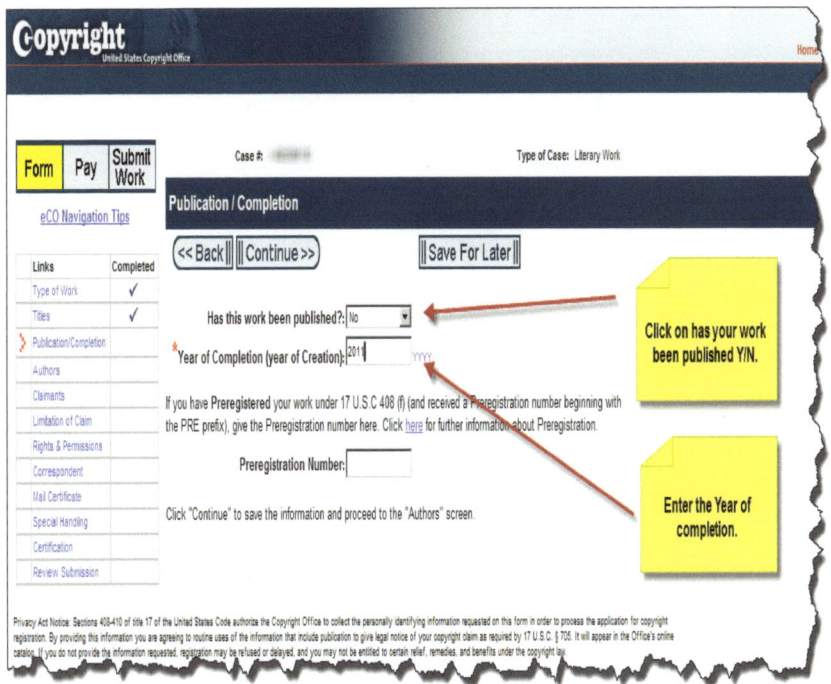

20) Fill in the author's name or add the organization's name. Make sure you fill in the asterisk information listed below.

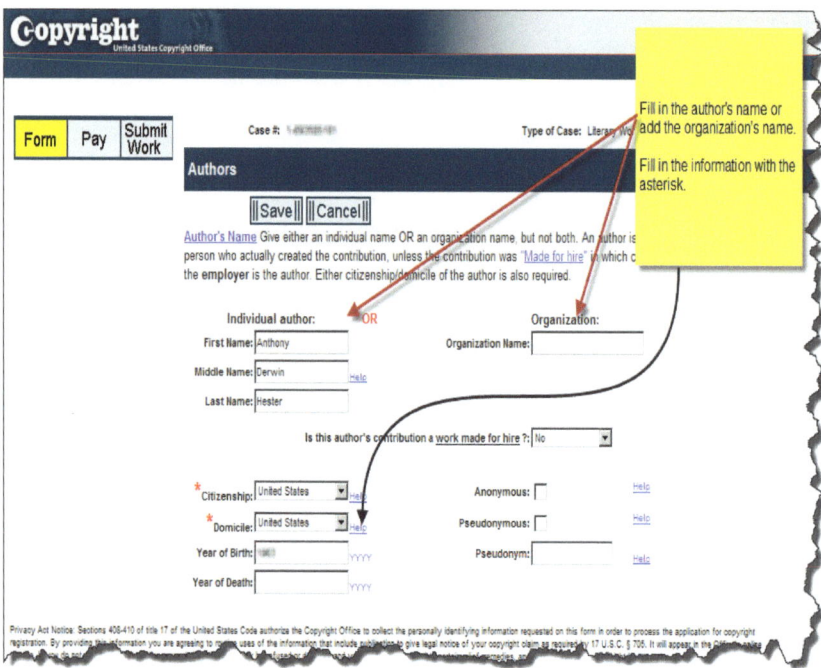

21) On this screen click on the box below that best describes the work that you created. If you have any questions click on the help button to the right side of the word, then click save.

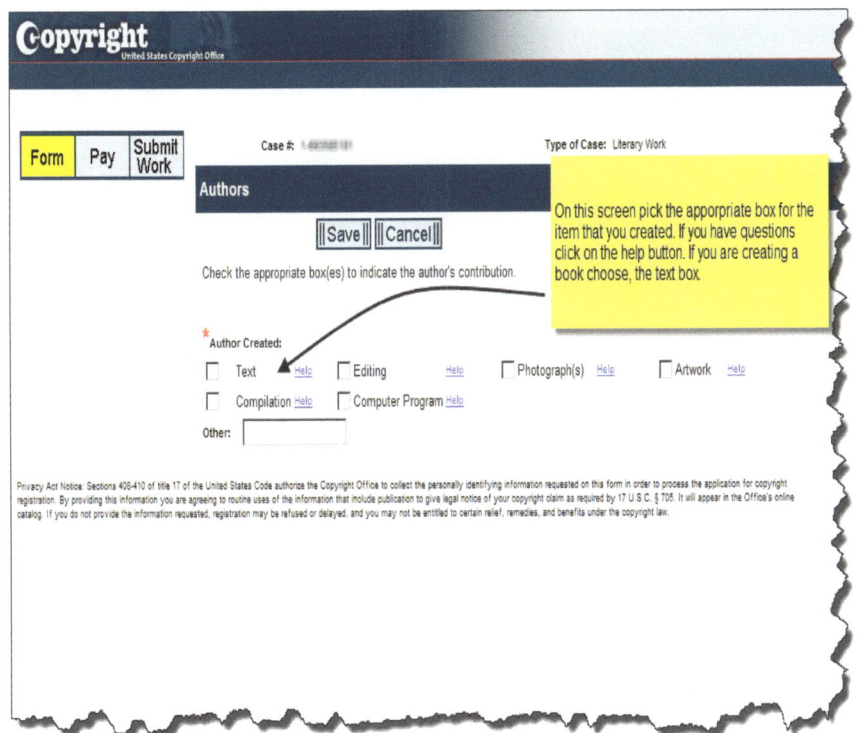

22) Claimants section:

If you are the only claimant click on Add Me. If you are not the only claimant click on the New button and add the different names.

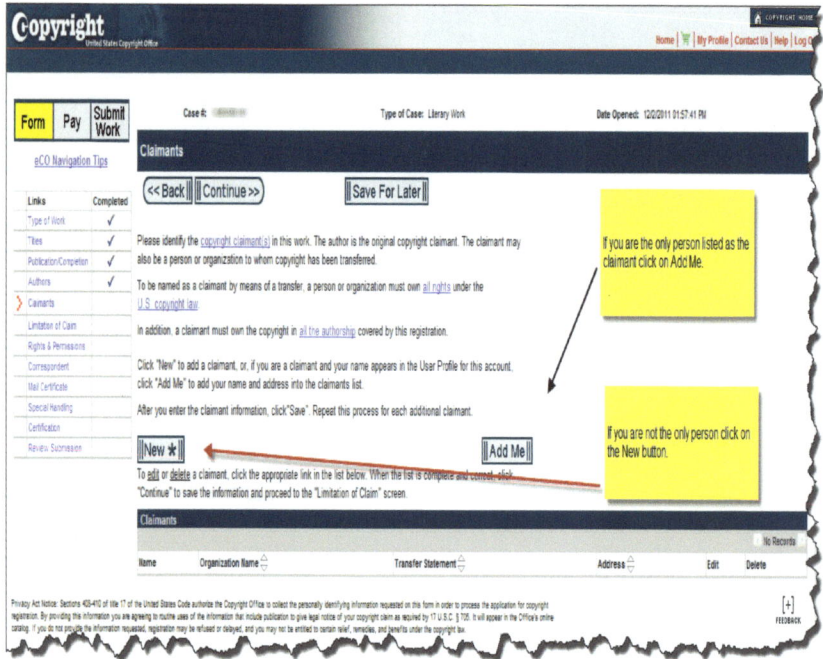

23) Limitation of claim:

In this section if your work does not contain any preexisting material click "Continue." If have any questions click on the section listed on the screen, "Limit your claim.

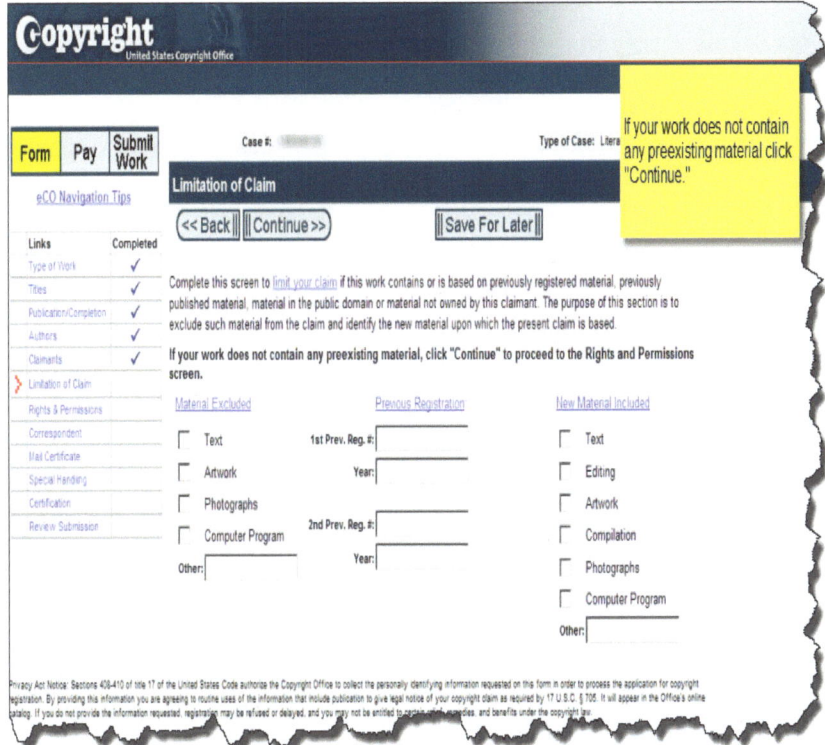

24) Right and Permission

Information (Optional) on this screen if you would like to leave information for a person or a group to contact you to request permission to use some or part of your completed work. Simply skip this step by clicking on the continue button.

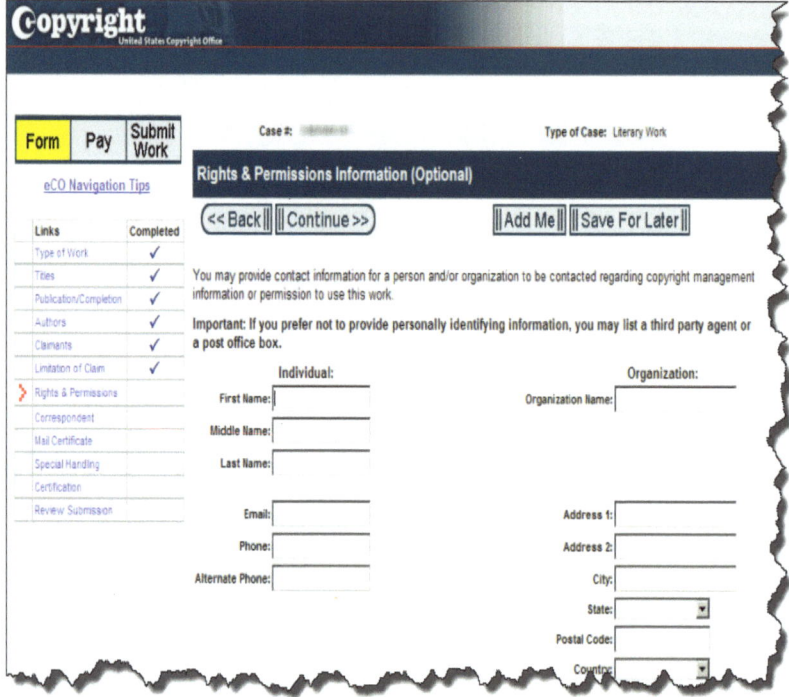

25) Correspondent Section:

Add your contact information so that if the Copyright office needs to contact you they will have your information.

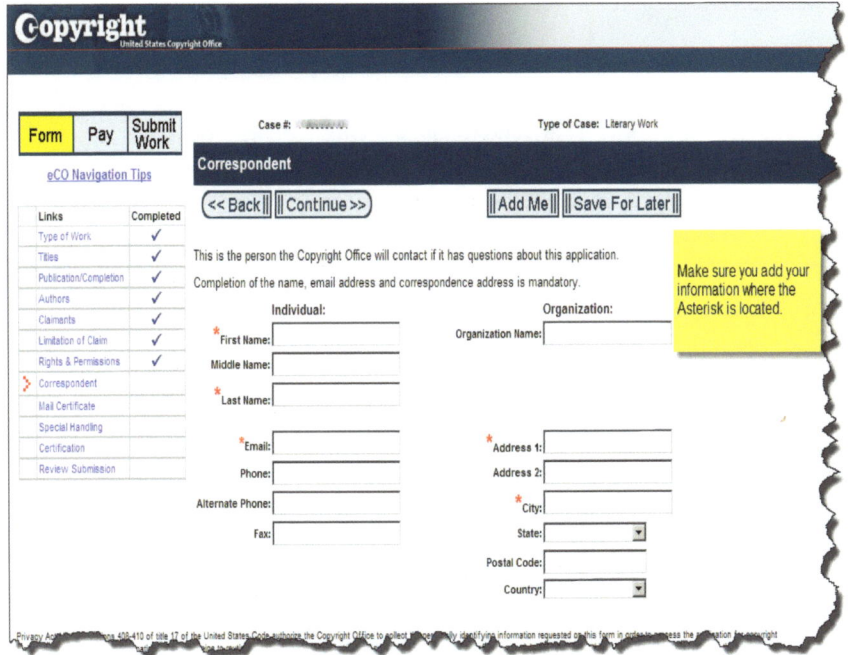

26) Mail Certificate:

27) Special Handling:

A Special Handling fee of $760 will expedite your application process claim within five working days. If your are not in a hurry just click continue.

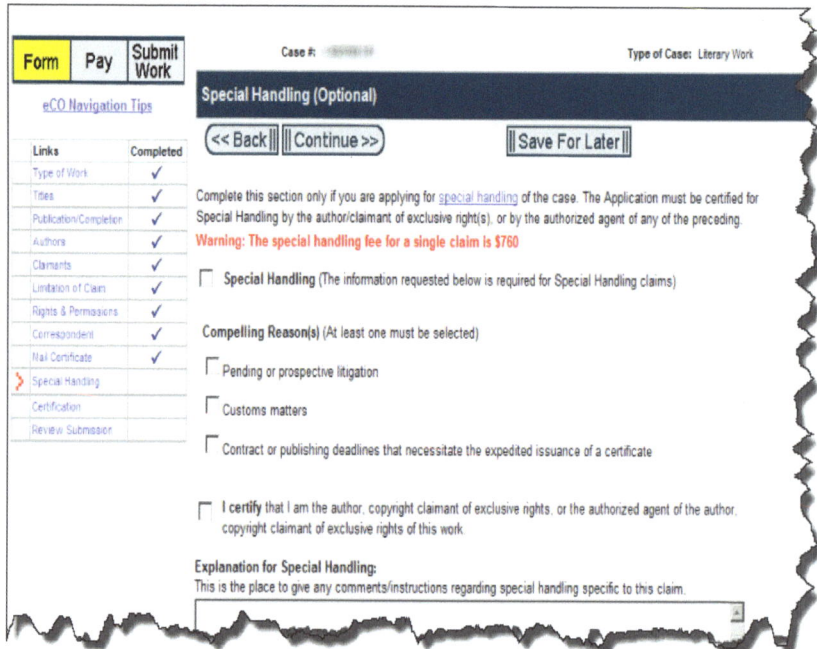

28) Certification:

The next screen is to certify as the authorized Author or the authorized Agent. Click on the box on the left, I Certify.

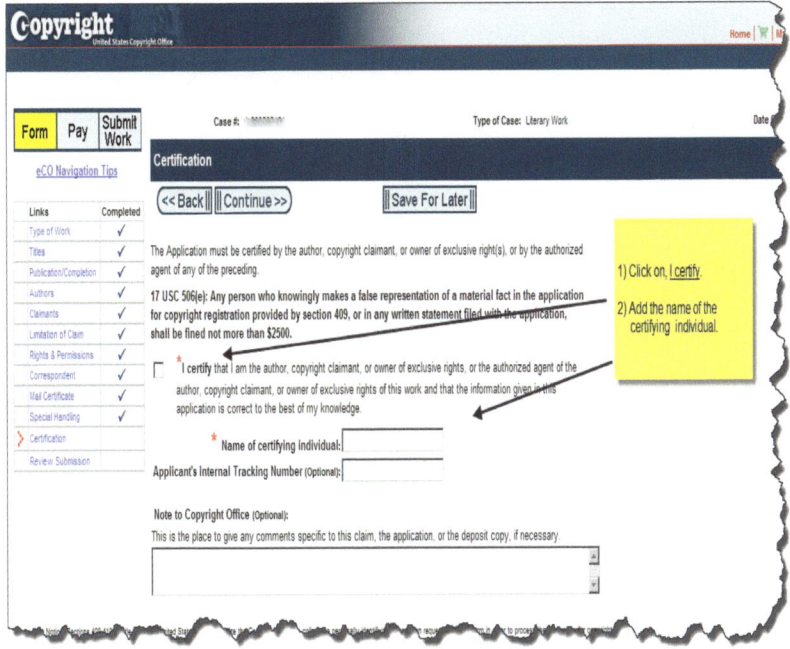

29) Review Submission:

The review submission screen will allow you to review your information prior to submitting your copyright application. Remember that this is your final chance to edit your information. Once you have proofed your work click on the add to cart button.

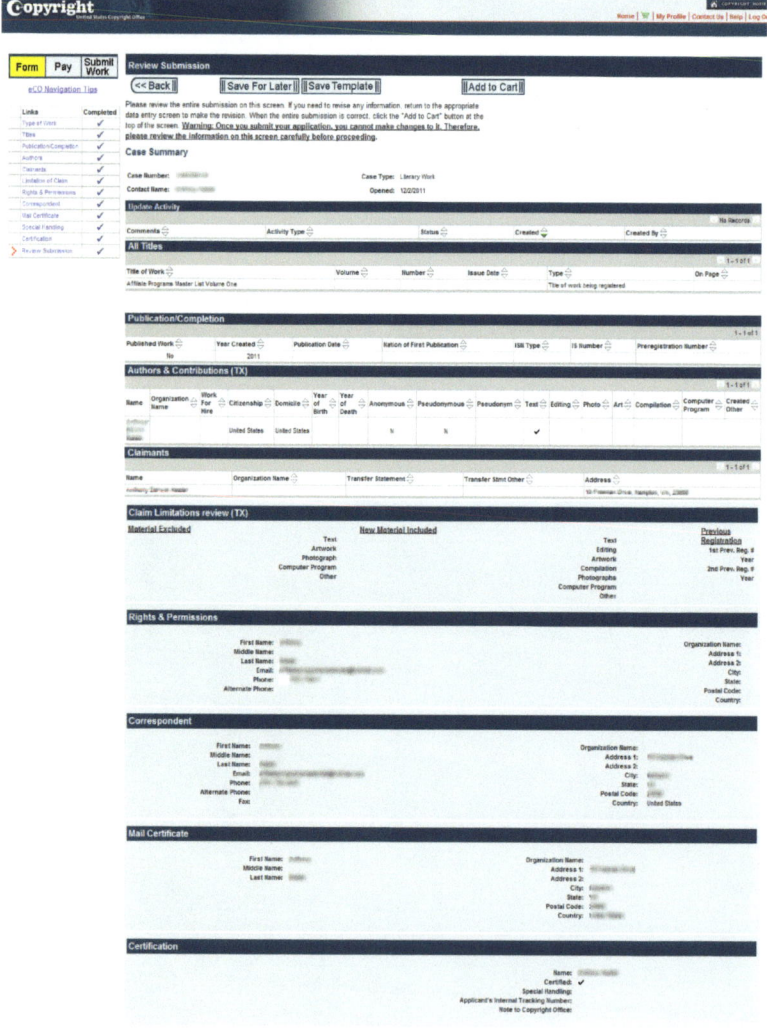

30) My cart:

My cart will show you all the filing fees. Click on the checkout button.

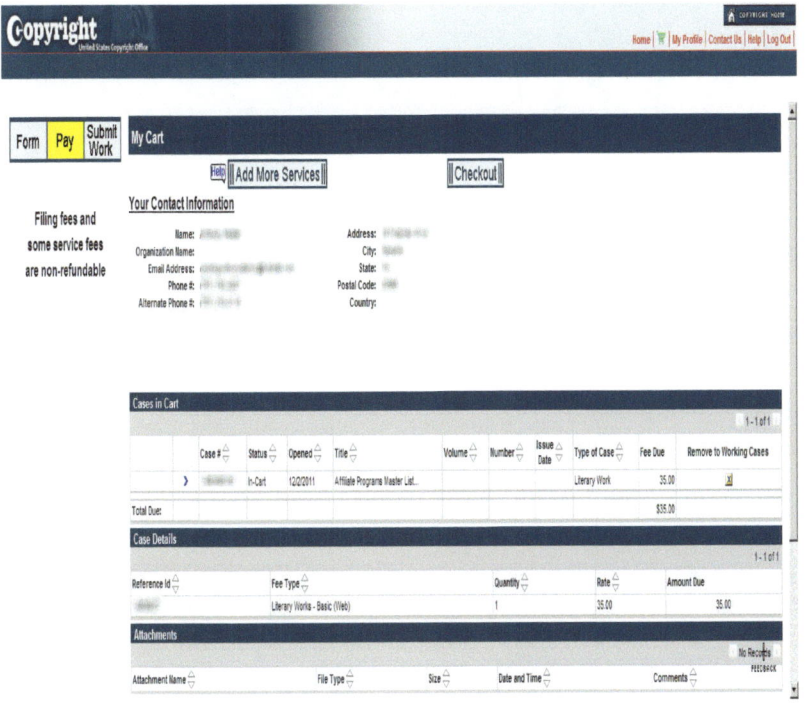

31) My Cart cont.

This screen allows you to choose a payment option.

32) This screen is letting you know that you are now leaving the Copyright office site and entering the U.S. Treasury to make your payment. Click, OK.

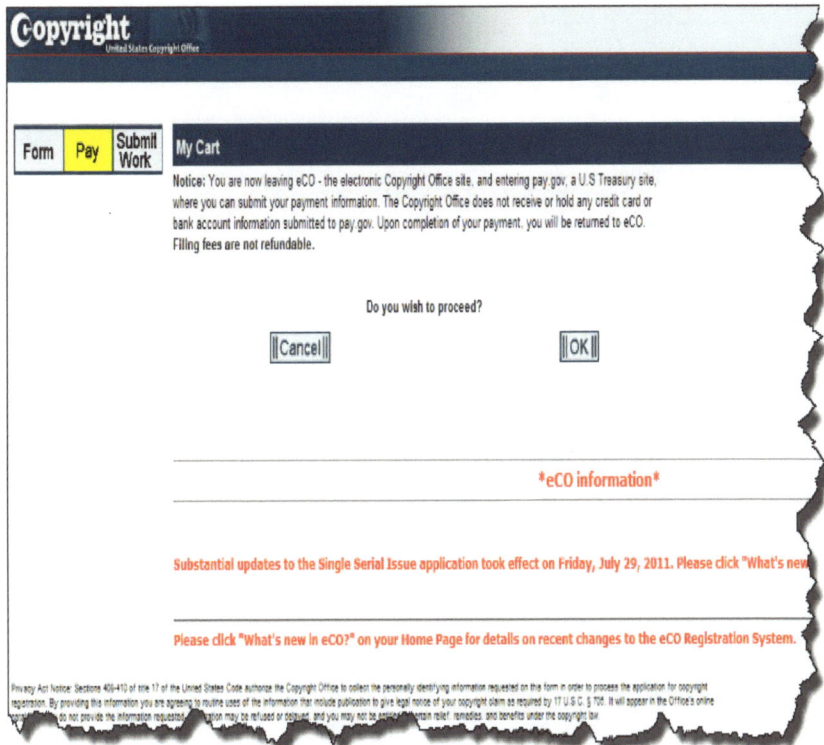

33) This allows you to select the method of payment. You have the option to pay by check or credit card.

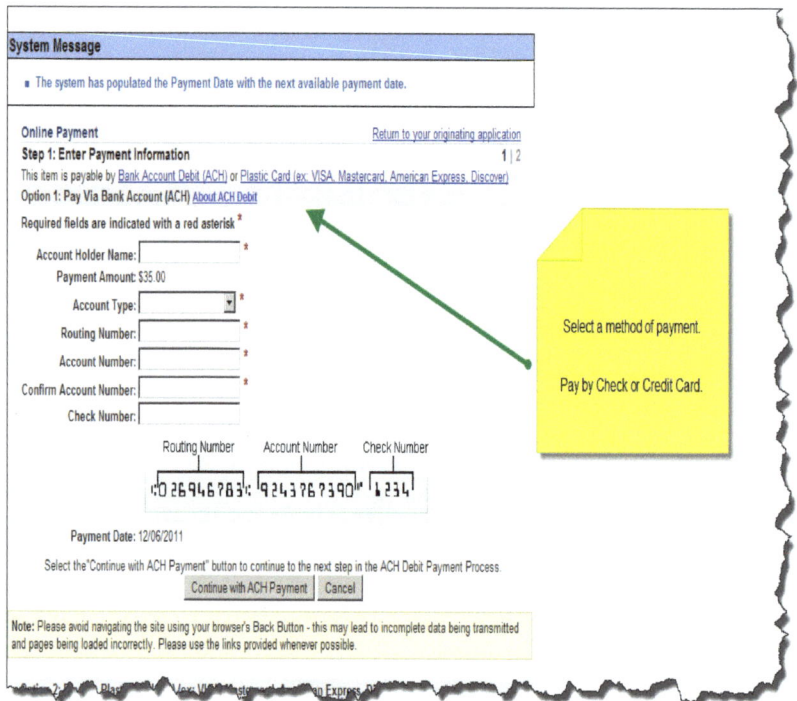

34) On this screen you can enter your credit card information. Then click on continue with Plastic Card Payment.

35) Put your email address in the email address field. The click on the box to the left of the asterisk to authorize payment. Then click on the Submit Payment button only once.

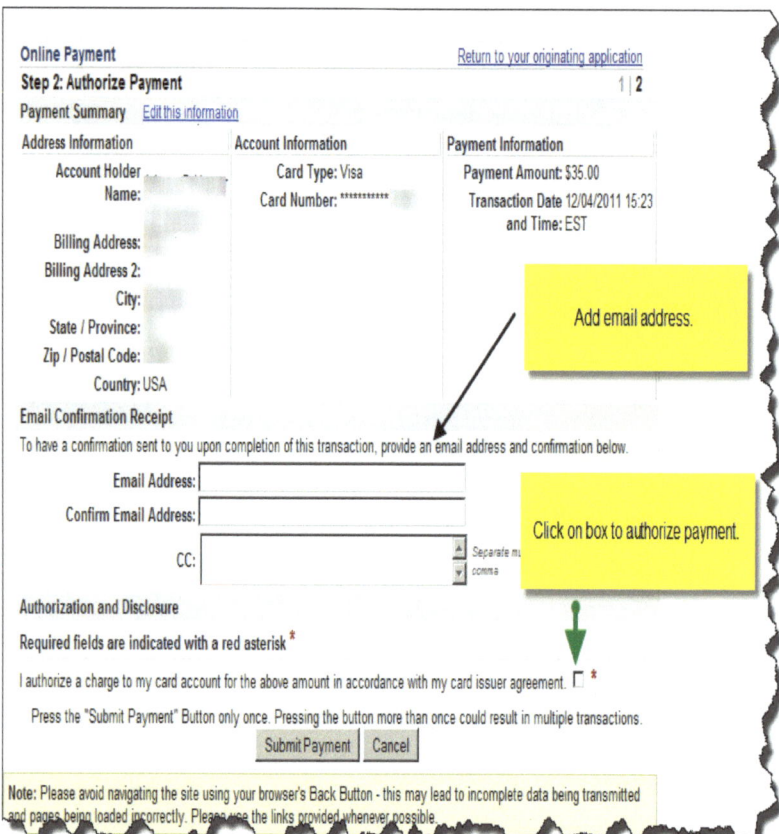

36) The next screen will state that the payment transaction was successful. Then click continue.

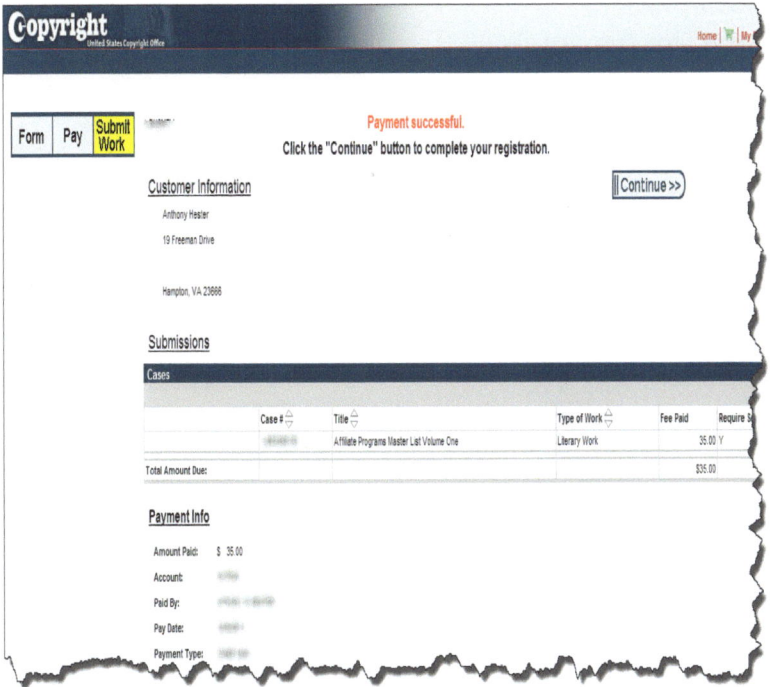

37) Electronic Upload:

You have two options on how to send your intellectual property to the Copyright Office.

1) Send your intellectual property via electronic upload.
2) Send it by mail.

In my case I have created an ebook using a word processing program and I sent the file via electronic transfer. I have used option two by sending by mail and using the shipping slip provided at the completion of the copyright approval. I have mailed motion pictures, audiovisual work, DVD's and DVD covers.

38) Upload Deposit:

Click on the Upload Deposit to browse and locate the electronic file to send to the Copyright Office. Once you find your file highlight then click open. Type a brief description of your work under the file. When you have finish that click on submit file to the Copyright Office. After a successful upload click close window. Note: If you plan on mailing your property click on, Create Shipping Slip.

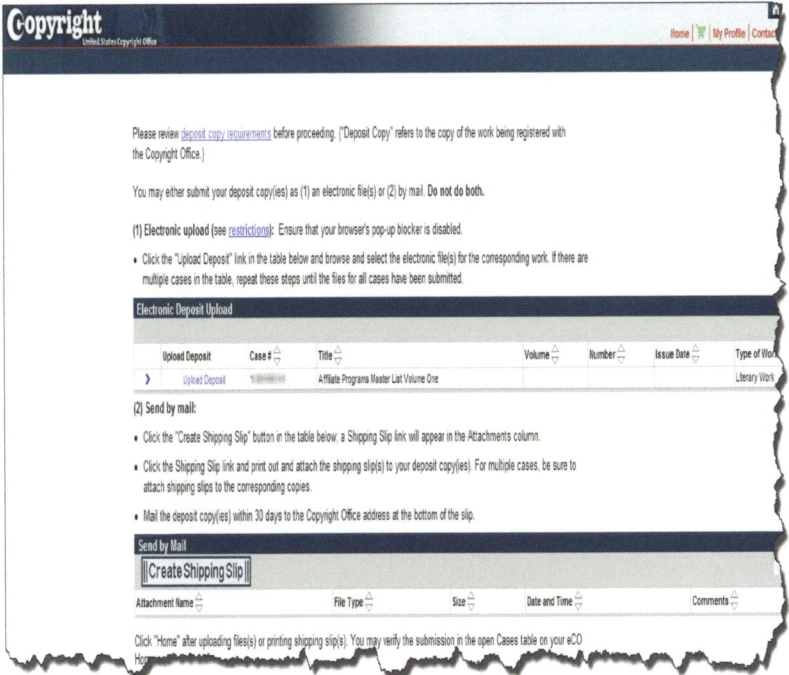

39) Your claim has been uploaded and updated. Keep your eyes open for future emails from the Copyright Office with special request and respond as soon as possible.

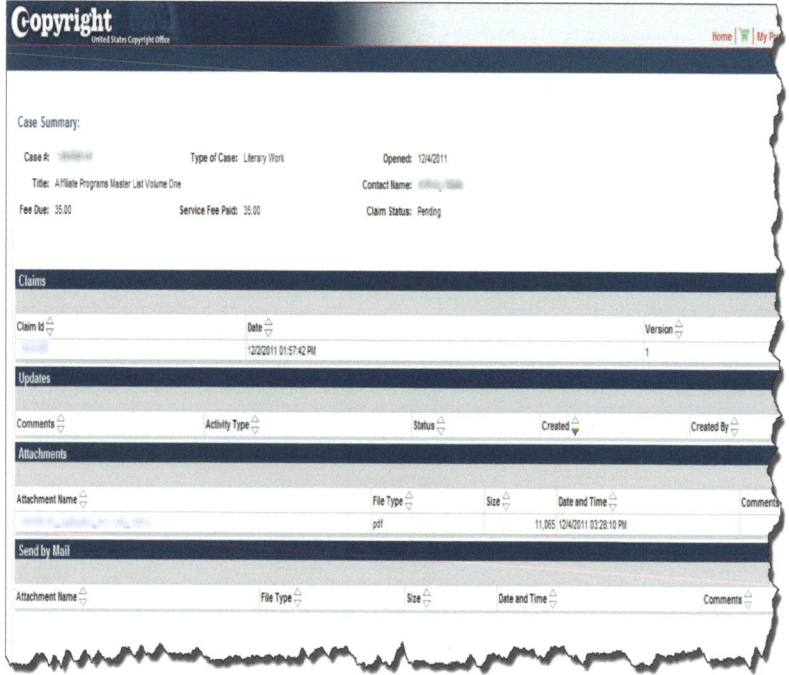

40) Now just seat back and relax the hard part is done. Before you know it the certificate for your copyright will arrive in the mail. The book created in this follow along example was approved. Titled: Affiliate Programs Master List by Anthony Hester.

Visit the link below to create quality custom products.
http://goo.gl/AcG0R

Also available from Anthony Hester
Affiliate Programs Master List

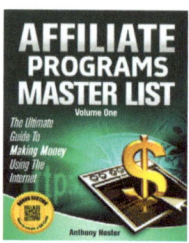

The Ultimate Guide To Making Money Using The Internet.

Up-to-date list (2012) of affiliate programs and products that you can market creating several streams of income from different sources.

You'll learn:
How to start an online business in less than one hour, FREE! Affiliate Programs (Brief Description of the Affiliate Companies) *Bonus section on How to create your own QR Codes ($300 Value) *List of over One Hundred Affiliate Marketing Programs. (Alphabetical order)

The Master Affiliate Program is your hands on guide to creating several streams of income. The e-book covers Affiliate programs such as Clickbank, Best Buy, AllPosters and much, much, more!

Create a business online for FREE! You don't have to pay any money to get started and the company will allow you to market your product via e-mail, Facebook, Twitter.

Not only can you sell your own products, but you can also sell other business owners products as well.

Get Started Today!

      Available from Amazon.com and other retailers.

Deep Frying Turkeys

Your Step-by-Step Guide to Deep Frying Turkeys

Learn how to safely make a Deep Fried Turkey! Cooking a turkey in this way can be quite dangerous if you don't know what you're doing, but it can be juicy and fantastic when done right. This DVD contains easy to understand directions, a scrumptious marinade recipe and everything you'll ever need to know about deep frying a turkey! Cooking With Uncle Tony shows you how with this Step-by-Step Guided video, going through important Safety Tips, Cooking Times, Cooking Temperatures, Recipe, Setting up the Deep Fryer and so much more! We're an Award Winning BBQ Team and we want to help you. Your guests deserve nothing but the best!

Stuffed Jalapeno Peppers

Your Step-by-Step Guide to Stuffed Jalapeno Peppers

Learn how to grill or roast your own Stuffed Jalapeno Peppers, perfect for parties or family gatherings! This DVD contains easy to understand directions, a scrumptious marinade recipe and everything you ever wanted to know about how to make delicious Stuffed Jalapeno Peppers! Cooking With Uncle Tony shows you how with this Step-by-Step Guided video, going through important Safety Tips, Cooking Times, Simple Tips for Stuffing Peppers, Cooking Temperatures, Choice of Fruit Woods, Recipe, Preparing the Smoker, How to Cook Them on the Grill or in an Oven and so much more! We're an Award Winning BBQ Team and we want to help you. Your guests deserve nothing but the best!

Smoked Turkey

Your Step-by-Step Guide to Smoked Turkey

Learn how to cook a delicious Smoked Turkey! This DVD contains easy to understand directions, a scrumptious marinade recipe and everything you ever wanted to know about how to BBQ one fantastic turkey! Cooking With Uncle Tony shows you how with this Step-by-Step Guide, going through important Safety Tips, Cooking Times, Cooking Temperatures, Choice of Fruit Woods, Recipe, Preparing the Smoker and so much more! We're an Award Winning BBQ Team and we want to help you. Your guests deserve nothing but the best!

Available at www.cookingwithuncletony.com

Created by:
Cooking With Uncle Tony, LLC
Award Winning BBQ Team

http://www.cookingwithuncletony.com/

Use your smartphone
to scan this code for a
direct connection or visit
(USE SCANLIFE APP)

Visit the link below to create **quality custom products.**
http://goo.gl/AcG0R

Copyright © 2012, Anthony D. Hester

www.ingramcontent.com/pod-product-compliance
Lightning Source LLC
Chambersburg PA
CBHW041110180526
45172CB00001B/194